Original title:
The Fruit's Journey

Copyright © 2025 Creative Arts Management OÜ
All rights reserved.

Author: Milo Harrington
ISBN HARDBACK: 978-1-80586-458-5
ISBN PAPERBACK: 978-1-80586-930-6

Bounty Beneath the Boughs

In shadows deep, where critters creep,
The apples hide, while squirrels peep.
A pear in suit, thinks it's so cute,
But can't escape that juicy loot!

The cherries laugh, they dance and shake,
While lemons scheme, for goodness' sake!
"Let's roll away," the berries play,
But stuck they are, every single day!

Orchard's Secret Pathways

Through twisted branches, paths do twine,
A grape on vine sways like fine wine.
Bananas slip, they often trip,
In silly games, they lose their grip!

The mango's sly, with a wink so spry,
It ducks and dives, oh my, oh my!
Citrus squawks, while laughter rocks,
As apples tell their gag-filled talks!

Fruitful Endeavors

The watermelon dreams of becoming a hat,
While oranges roll, no care in the spat.
"Catch me if you can!" the berries cheer,
But they end up stuck, year after year!

Avocados plot in a guacamole spree,
While cucumbers cling to their last bit of glee.
With every slice, a chuckle ensues,
In this fruity world, who would refuse?

The Kinship of Seeds

Seeds whisper softly, secrets untold,
In a veggie crew, both brave and bold.
A nutty affair with pistachios grand,
Makes even the dullest of carrots a brand!

As sprouts break free with a giggling shout,
"We're growing up!" they jiggle about.
Tomatoes wink, it's all a tease,
In this garden party, all are at ease!

In the Orchard's Breath

A pear on a branch did a jig,
Swaying to tunes from a plucky fig.
"Let's roll down the hill!" it exclaimed with glee,
But tripped on its leaves, oh what a sight to see!

The apples were laughing, oh what a scene,
A grape started dancing, so sprightly and keen.
They tossed all their seeds in a wild little game,
As pumpkins just sat, feeling rather lame.

Bananas were slipping, their peels in a pile,
While cherries were giggling, with bright little smiles.
A peach told a joke, it was juicy and sweet,
Limes mustered laughter, their zest was complete!

In orchards so merry, the laughter did flow,
Each fruit had a story, a bright tale to show.
With laughter and cheer, they all knew their fate,
Just hanging around, it's a fruity fate!

Fertile Whispers of Life

In the garden of fun, cucumbers sway,
A chorus of veggies, now leading the play.
Tomatoes in tutus, they spin with delight,
While onions discreetly poke fun out of sight.

The carrots are gossiping, heads held up high,
"Did you hear about corn? It's all ears," they cry.
Potatoes are rolling, all muddy and round,
They laugh at the peppers, all dressed in red gown.

"Let's throw a grand party!" a squash shouted loud,
While lettuce just sighed, feeling shy of the crowd.
Beets mixed their colors, a rainbow on show,
As radishes blushed at the attention they'd grow.

With whispers of life, in the soil they twist,
Each veggie a player, in the fun they exist.
In the fertile expanse, under sunshine so bright,
Together they flourish, in laughter's pure light!

Nature's Palette

In a garden of colors, oh what a sight,
Green peas in pajamas, feeling just right.
Tomatoes in tuxes, all dressed up to play,
While carrots giggle in their orange ballet.

Berries on swings, laughing with glee,
Dancing around like it's fruit jubilee.
Lemons start limbering, ready to roll,
While a cucumber juggles, striving for goal.

The Orchard's Hidden Narratives

Deep in the orchard, tales are spun,
Pears plotting mischief, just having fun.
Apples are whispering secrets of old,
Of pirates and treasure, as they unfold.

A grape, quite haughty, claims he's the best,
While cherries each claim they're totally blessed.
Lemons hold court, sassy and keen,
While a shy little peach peeks from the green.

Harvested Dreams

Under the sun, dreams ripen and bloom,
Pumpkin's a poet, with rhymes that go boom.
Radishes racing, with roots in a whirl,
While zucchinis plot, each one a twirl!

With laughter and cheer, they gather in bands,
Swaying and giggling, just holding hands.
On the farm, they dance, with joy in each sway,
Harvesting antics at the end of the day.

A Seed's Soliloquy

Oh, tiny seed, what wonders you hold,
Dreams of growing, both brave and bold.
With dirt on your face, you shout out in glee,
"I'll sprout into something, just wait and see!"

You shiver with laughter, through rain and through light,
Imagining flowers dressed in pure white.
A daisy in shades, can you hear her schemes?
Let the world chuckle at our leafy dreams!

Where Growing Dreams Blossom

In the garden, dreams sprout wide,
Bananas giggle as they slide.
Tomatoes blushing, feeling bold,
Whispering secrets, tales retold.

Carrots dance under the moon,
Radishes hum a cheerful tune.
Peppers joking from their vines,
Plotting pranks with witty signs.

The Orchard's Heartbeat

Apples grinning on the trees,
Mocking bees with silly tease.
Pears swing in a playful breeze,
Chasing shadows, oh, what a tease!

Cider dreams with laughter mixed,
Cherries plotting to be fixed.
Peachy puns that just won't quit,
Waiting for the perfect hit.

Nature's Culinary Journey

Lemons squabble in a bowl,
Pineapples generally on a roll.
Grapes debating on their hue,
Orange zest has a grand view.

Spinach just can't keep a straight face,
Broccoli's playing a vibrant race.
Radishes blush, oh so red,
While cucumbers giggle in bed.

In Search of the Sun

Berry brigade on a quest anew,
Chasing sunlight, just like you!
Strawberries wear their sun hats bright,
Singing songs of sweet delight.

Watermelon rolls with a grin,
Seeking rays where fun begins.
Avocados lounge, soaking up sun,
Whisp'ring tales of win and fun.

The Path of Ripening

In the orchard, a berry twirls,
Singing songs of juicy swirls.
Hanging tight on the vine's embrace,
Dreaming of a pie, a cozy place.

An apple struts with a shiny grin,
"Catch me if you can!" it shouts with spin.
A pear whispers tales of rustling leaves,
While a grape plots daring, sweet mischief he weaves.

A Voyage in Juices

A citrus crew sets sail with zest,
On a boat of pulp, they all invest.
Lemon leads with a tangy shout,
Orange rolls, "No doubt, no doubt!"

The blender churns like a wild old sea,
As they laugh and blend, "Oh, what fun to be!"
A splash of laughter, a sprinkle of cheer,
In their fruity chaos, there's nothing to fear.

Blossoms to Bowls

From sunny blooms, their history starts,
As bees bring news, with buzzing hearts.
"Rise and shine!" a banana declares,
While a lemon juggles, without a care.

From branch to bowl, they make a dash,
In a fruity frenzy, splattering splash.
With giggling seeds and succulent skins,
Every bite bursts with laughter that spins.

Nature's Sweet Odyssey

In the breeze, a peach rolls free,
Claiming adventure, "Just watch me!"
A cherry chuckles, "I'm quite the catch,"
While berries burst, a playful batch.

Through gardens wide, they frolic and play,
Each fruit dreams big, come what may.
In a salad giggle, all flavors unite,
"Let's dance on the plate!" they cheer with delight.

Rhythm of the Seasons

In spring they start to dance and sing,
A wobbly fruit doing its thing.
Summer sun, oh so bright,
Turns green apples to a shiny sight.

Autumn's wind gives them a whirl,
Spinning around with a twist and a twirl.
The winter chill? Not a scare,
Just cozying up, a fruit affair!

Sunkissed and Sown

Under the sun, they bask with glee,
Wiggling on vines, oh what a spree!
With a wink to the breeze, they share a joke,
As they ripen up, just like a poke.

Planted with care in the rich, soft dirt,
They giggle and squirm, covered in shirt.
From seed to snack, what a delight,
Snack time's fun, ready for a bite!

From Petal to Plate

Once a petal, soft and sweet,
Now a pie, oh what a treat!
They laugh as they roll on the counter with grace,
Heading to plates for a sugary race.

Flour flies as they take a leap,
In the oven, they start to creep.
Out they come, a golden gang,
Telling stories of how they sang!

The Art of Growing

A sprout popped up, thought it was cool,
'Hey, I'm the king of this leafy school!'
Roots wiggled under, feeling so bold,
They whispered secrets in moist, dark mold.

With a splash of rain, they giggle and sway,
Every drop a party in a glorious way!
Branches stretch out to make more friends,
Laughing together as each day ends.

Seeds of Adventure

Once I was a tiny seed,
Hiding in the ground, oh indeed.
Wiggling worms would pass me by,
I'd giggle, thinking, 'Oh my, oh my!'

A sunbeam hit my sheltered face,
I sprouted fast, picked up the pace.
With roots below and shoots above,
I waved to clouds and swayed with love.

Bouncing bugs would cheer me on,
'You're growing up, you're never gone!'
I danced with breezes, laughed with rain,
A tiny hero, no room for pain!

Now I'm a tree, a sight to see,
With branches wide, come climb with me!
Let's have a picnic on my leaves,
And tell the tales of growing dreams!

From Blossom to Bounty

In spring I bloomed all pink and white,
A buzzing bee came for a bite.
He swirled around, thought he'd won,
But I just laughed, 'You're outdone!'

Petals danced in the gentle breeze,
It tickled my stems, oh what a tease!
A little breeze, a little sway,
I cheered, 'Who knew I'd have such a day?'

Through sunny days, I grew so proud,
In summer's warmth, I laughed aloud.
Fruits formed like beads, hanging tight,
Just wait, dear friends, for my big night!

The harvest came, they filled their bags,
With juicy bites and happy jags.
I giggled loud as I watched them cheer,
What fun to be a fruit, oh dear!

Whispers of Orchard Tales

Under an apple tree so stout,
The squirrels chatted, running about.
'Have you heard the news?' one said,
'Bob the peach is turning red!'

The pears were gossiping each day,
'Have you noted how the grapes sway?'
They'd share their dreams and silly jokes,
Each branch full of laughing folks!

A cherry tried to sing a tune,
But slipped and fell down with a swoon.
'Watch your step!' the others cried,
While fruit friends giggled, side by side.

At twilight when the sun was low,
Orchard tales began to flow.
With laughter echoing through the night,
Fruits shared their secrets, what a sight!

Harvesting Dreams

The farmer's hat was tall and grand,
He waved his flag, made a stand.
'Gather 'round, let's start the fun,
It's harvest time, go, go, run!'

We rolled and tumbled in the dirt,
Avoiding bees, oh what a spurt!
'Grab a basket, fill it fast,
Let's pick these fruits, it'll be a blast!'

With every peach tucked snug and warm,
We laughed at fruit flies, 'Oh what charm!'
The apples giggled, hiding away,
'How many more can we sway?'

As twilight wrapped the day in dreams,
We feasted under starlit beams.
With happy hearts and juicy schemes,
We savored life, and endless gleams!

The Sweetness Unfolds

In the orchard, the apples giggle,
Pears jump around, doing a wiggle.
Bananas slip on peels so bright,
They jest in the sun, what a sight!

Cherries dance in the gentle breeze,
Strawberries pose with flair and tease.
Oranges roll, a silly race,
Lemonade dreams in a cheerful place.

Grapes gossip under viney halls,
Whispering secrets, oh how it sprawls!
Each one a joker, a vine-dressed clown,
Their laughter echoes, never a frown.

With every bite, a burst of cheer,
Fruits unite, spreading good cheer.
Sweetness unfolds, hilarity abounds,
In the land of snacks, joy resounds!

A Caramelized Chronicle

From the tree, a peach took flight,
With a scoop of ice cream, what a sight!
Caramel drips, a sticky affair,
Grinning as it glides through the air.

Plums in a pot, swirling around,
Figs in pajamas, all tightly bound.
A dash of humor, sprinkle of fun,
Bouncing in bowls, oh what a run!

Coconut jokes with a chocolate twist,
Whipped cream grins, you can't resist.
Fruit salad tales, a blend so bright,
Each spoonful's laughter, pure delight.

Redirecting drumsticks, all meant to sway,
The caramel's laughter will steal the day.
With a fruity twist, life's a parade,
Join the fun, don't let it fade!

Routes of the Harvest

Through fields of green, they take their stand,
A bunch of berries, hand in hand.
Potatoes rolling, trying to race,
Carrots hop, with roots in place.

Onion layers, they try to hide,
While broccoli acts like it's certified.
Tomatoes chuckle, red as can be,
A veggie vignette, oh what glee!

Pumpkins jest, their jokes so corny,
While radishes blush, feeling thorny.
Each path they wander, a caper unfolds,
As nature's bounty, entertainingly bold!

Fruits and veggies on this ludicrous ride,
Gathering tales with nothing to hide.
Harvesting laughter, in every twist,
Join the convoy, you won't want to miss!

.

Nature's Tasty Pilgrimage

Berries bounce down the road so spry,
While kiwis do backflips, oh my, oh my!
Pineapples giggle, wearing their crown,
While mangoes spin, twirling around.

In a picnic basket, a grape brigade,
Rolling and tumbling, a fruity parade.
With a splash of lemon giving a cheer,
It's a journey of flavor, sincere and dear.

Watermelon's laughter makes puddles of pink,
As citrus friends plot and think.
They toast to summer, so fresh, so bright,
In nature's pageant, it's sheer delight!

Gathering stories from each sunny day,
On this adventure, come join the play!
Nature's tasty pilgrimage, always a thrill,
With every bite, it's laughter to fill!

Born from Earth's Embrace

In a field of dirt and sun,
Little seeds just want some fun.
With a wiggle and a dance,
Up they pop, their chance to prance.

With a splash of rain delight,
They grow roots and stretch up tight.
Leaves high-five in the soft breeze,
While critters dance among the peas.

The sun laughs with a bright cheer,
As flowers bloom, they're all in gear.
"Look at us," they sing so proud,
Dancing 'neath the fluffy cloud.

Then comes a squirrel, here to steal,
"I'm just tasting, it's no big deal!"
They giggle as they turn to round,
Nature's party all around.

Colors of Autumn's Offering

The leaves are falling, what a sight,
Red and gold, they twirl in flight.
An apple shouts, "Come join the spree!"
"Catch me if you can," says he.

Pumpkins play a game of hide,
In the patch, they swell with pride.
"Guess my weight," they shout aloud,
Laughter echoes from the crowd.

Grapes hang low, all tight and round,
"I'm a cluster, can't be found!"
Beneath a canopy of cheer,
They sip the sunshine throughout the year.

As the harvest brings a feast,
Everyone's giggling, not the least.
Thankful for the autumn's show,
We pick and munch and bask in glow.

A Taste of the Wild

In the forest, berries hide,
"Eat us!" they cheer, full of pride.
A rogue raccoon, sly and spry,
Nibbles fruit until he's shy.

Mushrooms giggle, dressed in spots,
"Pick us, but avoid the dots!"
With every twist and every turn,
The little critters laugh and learn.

A trail of nuts from tree to tree,
"Join the party, come and see!"
With every crunch, a juicy sound,
A feast of laughter all around.

Underneath the leafy shade,
Nature's fun, never to fade.
In this wild and wacky land,
Let's get lost, just take my hand.

The Path of the Orchard

Down the lane, the orchard calls,
With rows of fruit, against the walls.
Apples grin, and pears just sway,
"Who's coming for a fun-filled day?"

Cherries giggle, hanging tight,
"Let's roll down, oh what a sight!"
With every bounce, they land with glee,
"Oh my, this is wild, whee!"

The oranges try a silly dance,
While lemons join, not missing their chance.
"Let's twist and turn, we'll spin around!"
The laughter echoes, such joy is found.

As baskets fill with colors bright,
The orchard shines in pure delight.
In this sweet, delightful land,
Cheery fruits all take a stand.

From Root to Radiance

In the soil, they wiggle and giggle,
With visions of sunshine, they dance and swiggle.
Among the worms, they play hide and seek,
Rooting for laughter, the outcome is chic.

With a quick flip, they sprout out wide,
Out of the dark, with no place to hide.
They trump their way into daylight's embrace,
Chasing the sunshine, a zany race!

From green to red, what a silly affair,
Dressed up in colors, they beam with flair.
"Oh, I'm a peach, no wait, I'm a pear!"
Mismatched identities filling the air.

Then comes the taste, a fruity delight,
With laughter and giggles, oh what a sight!
Sharing their sweetness on plates is a blast,
Cheers to the fun, let's make it last!

This Sweet Evocation

A berry burst in a tiny blue car,
Zooming past cucumbers, oh they're bizarre.
They honk and shout, 'We're packed up tight!'
Bound for the kitchen, what a fruity flight!

The apples wear hats, all spruced up and bright,
While bananas slip in the laughter at night.
"Peel me a story!" the citrus will yell,
As the grapes just giggle and jibe in their shell.

Each fruit has a tale, a quirky charade,
From orchard to table, a grand masquerade.
"Let's party!" they cheer, with zest and good cheer,
In the bowl of delight, together they steer.

With a flash and a crunch, they dance on the plate,
Vibrant and zany, they celebrate fate.
A fruity fiesta, with smiles all around,
This sweet evocation, where joy can be found.

Nature's Palette Unveiled

In gardens so wild, the colors collide,
With carrots in capes taking vegetables' pride.
Tomatoes are blushing, feeling so grand,
While peas play tricks, oh isn't it grand!

The lemons are laughing with sunshiny glee,
As limes join the chorus, oh can't you see?
Cantaloupes giggle in orange-hued dreams,
Splashing the world with their fruity schemes.

"Look out for the flavor!" shouts mango with zest,
While cherries sport crowns, feeling the best.
So vivid, so charming, the fruit's little show,
Nature's palette unveiled, oh what a glow!

From garden to table, they roll with delight,
Painting the world with their taste, pure and light.
With every bite taken, it's laughter and bliss,
In this colorful banquet, you can't miss!

Mosaic of Edibles

A patchwork of colors, the fruit bowl's a sight,
Berries are giggling, all merry and bright.
Grapefruits perform pirouettes, so spry,
While apples crack jokes that make everyone cry.

"Who hired the juice?" asks banana, quite bold,
As oranges tease in their jackets of gold.
Together they dance in a splatter of jams,
Creating a symphony, oh, what a clams!

In this mosaic, where flavors unite,
Every piece has a story, each bite feels just right.
With laughter like bubbles that float in the air,
Fruits share their secrets, and joy is laid bare.

From market to kitchen, they jive and they play,
Creating a masterpiece fresh every day.
In a bowl of edibles, fun's never shy,
Grab a spoon, take a dive, give joy a try!

Gentle Hands and Green Thumbs

In a garden so bright, with veggies in sight,
Benny the tomato, he plays hide and seek.
With a tickle of leaves, and a taste of delight,
He giggles aloud—"I'm juicy, not weak!"

Carrot's got jokes, he's the clown of the patch,
Telling all the radishes, "I'm a real catch!"
With his green tops all bouncy, they dance till they scratch,
"In salads we shine, we're quite the great match!"

Cucumbers whisper, "Let's roll in the dirt,"
They tumble and giggle, all muddy and flirts.
"We're meant for the pickles, they'll give us a spurt!"
As they splash through the puddles, their laughter converts.

Peppers, in colors, from yellow to red,
Form a conga line, as they jive ahead.
Spicy and sweet, in a fiesta, they spread,
"We're the life of the party, just look where we tread!"

Echoes of Earth's Warmth

There once was a berry, with dreams oh so bold,
He wanted to fly, not just sit in the cold.
"With wings made of sunshine, and hearts made of gold,
I'll soar like the birds, through the skies uncontrolled!"

So off he went bouncing, with gusto and flair,
He jumped on a leaf, took a leap through the air!
"Catch me if you can, I'm elusive, take care,
I'll wobbly-wobble, while you give yours a stare!"

But soon in the breeze, poor berry took a dive,
Into a fruit bowl, his dreams didn't arrive.
With apples and bananas, he learned to survive,
"Maybe I'm better, just keeping this vibe!"

Now he tells tales, to all in the bowl,
Of windy adventures, and how to be whole.
They laugh and they giggle, each fruit with a role,
Together they sing, the fruit-loving soul!

The Flavorful Quest

In a pantry so high, a secret they found,
A pie's grand adventure, that's world-renowned.
With crusts made of giggles, no one's ever frowned,
Each bite's an explosion, mouths are spellbound!

The apples declared, "We're on a crusade!",
To find the best spices, so nobody's paid.
Cinnamon joined in, with a swirl and a shade,
"Let's make it delightful, let sweetness invade!"

The cherries were hopping, all red and so plump,
"We'll throw in a dance, to give it a jump!"
A sprinkle of laughter, an ice cream lump,
For every new flavor, they'd just take a thump!

And when all was done, the pie took its stand,
"Join me at the table, come gather 'round,
With laughter and joy, we'll all make a band,
I'm the slice of the party, together we're grand!"

Harvested Moments

In the field where the pumpkins were rolling in cheer,
One pumpkin named Pete had a bright shining leer.
"I'm off to the town, make my debut here!"
He winked and he giggled, spreading good cheer.

The carrots were jealous, as they whispered and pouted,
"Don't leave us behind, we know we are doubted!"
But Pete just chuckled, his joy was well routed,
"Come along for the ride, you won't be outshouted!"

So, they hitched a big wagon, with all of their zest,
Chasing after dreams, they put friendship to test.
"We'll be legends together, we'll laugh with the best!"
As they rolled through the town, feeling truly blessed.

At the festival's end, with hearts filled with cheer,
They danced to the music, their laughter sincere.
"We made quite the memories, all throughout the year,
Gather 'round for the harvest, let's raise up a beer!"

From Shrub to Table

In the garden they grow with glee,
Hiding from squirrels, oh woe is me!
Sunshine and rain, a dance so spry,
"Don't eat me yet!" the berries cry.

Picking time comes with a jolly cheer,
"Not too ripe!" they shout in fear.
But off they go, into the bowl,
Planning their future, that's the goal!

A sprinkle of sugar, a dash of flair,
"Now we can finally go somewhere!"
Chased by forks, they roll and slip,
"Oh no, not that salad trip!"

Stirred and folded, what a delight,
From garden's edge, to here tonight,
Pies and jams, oh what a fable!
Who knew they'd end up on the table?

A Harvest of Echoes

In the orchard, a lively debate,
Whispers of apples determine their fate.
"Pick me first!" the loudest calls,
While the peaches just giggle in their stalls.

The pears form a line, oh what a sight,
"Let's outshine the apples, be merry and bright!"
But the veggies just shake their leafy heads,
"We're way too classy," they jokingly said.

Time for the harvest, let the fun begin,
In baskets they tumble, with raucous din.
Bouncing and laughing, they take a ride,
To the market where chaos and cheer collide.

Every fruit shouts, "Please pick me!"
While the melons dream of sweet jubilee.
All tangled together, an orchard parade,
Echoing laughter as freshness is made!

Sweetness in the Air

In the orchard trees, spirits high,
Buzzing with laughter, oh my, oh my!
With blossoms that sway and twirl with grace,
"Don't eat me yet," wears a playful face.

The bees buzz around with a jig so fine,
"Just a quick taste, we won't cross the line!"
Berries blush red in a sunny display,
"Save some for later," they cheekily say.

Bananas wear hats, while grapes find a friend,
"What's that over there? Is it time to blend?"
Smoothies and snacks dance in the air,
With flavors so funny, they banish despair!

From the tree-tops to kitchen fame,
Each one vying for a taste of the game.
Sweetness ensues in giggles and flair,
A garden of laughter, where joy is laid bare!

Metamorphosis of Flavor

Once a tiny seed, oh what a plan,
"I'll sprout a fruit!" it boldly ran.
From dirt to sunlight, a dream unfurling,
"Watch out world, I'm coming, twirling!"

Growing so tall, each day a surprise,
Bouncing with joy beneath sunny skies.
"I may be an oddball," the kiwi laughed,
"But wait 'til you taste my exotic craft!"

The pumpkins chuckle, "We'll become pies!"
While carrots whisper, "We'll win this prize!"
Each harvest a riddle, a twist of fate,
In the stew pot bubbling, they congregate!

What a wild ride from seed to delight,
With salads and sauces that take flight.
Each flavor a story, each bite a cheer,
Savoring silliness, bringing us near!

Tales of Vine and Branch

From vine to mouth, they make a dash,
Grapes giggle, slipping, what a splash!
With every twist, a berry cheers,
"Watch out, I'm ripe!" it boldly jeers.

Bananas toss in sunlit glee,
Chasing shadows, oh so free.
Peaches roll with a rosy grin,
"Is it my turn? Let the games begin!"

Lemons lemon-squeeze in delight,
Sour faces make the party bright.
Tomatoes squirt, a juice parade,
In this fruit fest, no one will fade.

Vines will dance 'neath the warm sun,
Swaying and laughing, oh what fun.
From garden bed to kitchen flair,
Fruit friends gather, none can compare!

Roots Beneath the Sky

Down below, in cozy dark,
Roots play tag, a playful lark.
"Who's the tallest?" they all boast,
But dirt's the place they'd rather host.

They stretch and wiggle with all their might,
To touch the sun, what a delight!
Yet, prancing pests thought they could tease,
Until the roots yelled, "Stop with ease!"

Worms bring snacks, a squirmy feast,
Pizza crust, oh, what a beast!
While up above, the fruits all grin,
"Keep digging deep, we'll never give in!"

Together they cheer beneath the glow,
In this earthy dance, roots put on a show.
All lined up, there's no fear in sight,
With silly shapes, what a funny fright!

Of Sunshine and Showers

Sunshine beams on apples bright,
Hats made of leaves, oh what a sight!
While clouds above begin to pout,
The fruits giggle, "Let it spout!"

Raindrops tap, a rhythm neat,
Fruits all dance with nimble feet.
"Slip and slide!" the berries cry,
"Splat! I'm wet!"—oh my, oh my!

Lemons laugh, all set for play,
Dancing puddles, come what may.
Blueberries bounce, in twirls they glide,
Making waves like a water slide!

When sun and rain join in a spree,
Colors pop, so wild and free.
Up there in nature's crazy game,
They show us life is never tame!

The Symphony of Harvest

In the orchard, a tune in the air,
Fruits harmonize without a care.
Apples hum, while pears go plop,
In this farmyard, no beat will stop.

The drummer's beat, a pumpkin rolls,
Mellow melodies with squashy goals.
Listen closely, the berries sing,
In this harvest, joy's the king!

Bananas swing like funky beats,
Twirling branches in joyous feats.
"You can't catch us!" cherries tease,
As they bounce on the autumn breeze.

The crops all cheer and make a ruckus,
Bursting with laughter, oh what a circus!
In this grand show, with nature's art,
The harvest's rhythm fills every heart!

A Tale of Sweetness

In the orchard, a peach was bold,
Claiming its throne, it felt so gold.
"I'm the sweetest!" it did proclaim,
While the apples giggled, "Oh, what a shame!"

A banana slipp'd, a comedic sight,
Caught in a dance, it slipped left and right.
"Peel me a joke, come join the fun!"
Laughter echoed, until the day was done.

Grapes formed a crew, just hanging tight,
They threw a party, oh what a sight!
"Whoever says raisins have the best taste?"
Was met with a burst of laughter, no haste.

With berries bright, they formed a band,
Strawberry strums, with raspberry fans.
Together they sang with juice-filled cheer,
In a world where sweetness brings no fear!

Nature's Gift Unfurled

In a garden lush, a carrot peeked,
"I'm not a fruit," it timidly squeaked.
But the tomatoes laughed, all squishy and round,
"You're part of the salad, so don't feel down!"

The lemons rolled in, with zest so bold,
"Sour is funny, just watch me unfold!"
With a twist and a turn, they did somersaults,
Making all veggies forget their faults.

A pumpkin sat proud, like a king on its throne,
"I'm the biggest!" it boomed with a groan.
But the cucumbers whispered, with cheeky grins,
"Size doesn't matter, it's how you spin!"

While dancing marigolds splashed colors around,
The veggies all tumbled, fell to the ground.
With laughter and glee, they embraced their fate,
Nature's odd bunch, it's never too late!

Beyond the Tree's Canopy

High in the branches, fruits had a show,
Mangoes swung low, with a breezy flow.
"Catch me if you can!" the cherries did cry,
As oranges rolled down, with a big, juicy sigh.

Pineapple tried to join in the race,
Wobbling awkwardly, it made such a face.
"I'm here for the snacks, but can't get the groove!"
So the others just laughed, and started to move.

Avocado was cool, with shades decked out,
"I'm smooth and I'm hip, without a doubt!"
But the apples just chuckled, in colors so bright,
"We're the real stars, shining all night!"

As the sun set low, they called it a day,
The fruits all agreed, it was fun in a way.
Under leaves' cover, they took to their dreams,
Of mischief and laughter, or so it seems!

The Dance of Pollination

Buzzing around, the bees had a ball,
Pollinating flowers, having a call.
"Dance with me, petals, we'll whirl and twirl!"
While the daisies laughed, with a comical swirl.

The butterflies fluttered, adorned with flair,
"Join our frolic, if you dare!"
But the roses just sighed, with a shake of their heads,
"We're busy blooming, no time for beds!"

A dandelion joked, with seeds on its hair,
"I'll fly away, if you want to spare!"
The bees all buzzed, with a hearty cheer,
"Float on, dear friend, we'll keep you near!"

Through the gardens, the laughter did bloom,
Nature's own circus, no trace of gloom.
With pollen in the air, and joy at its core,
The dance of the flowers was never a bore!

Between Trees and Tides

In the orchard, apples giggle,
Peaches float, quite the wiggle.
Bananas dance by the bay,
Lemons splash in a zesty way.

Grapes on vines like tiny jesters,
Bouncing forth, oh such testers.
Coconuts crack jokes with the sun,
While cherries cheer, 'We're just fun!'

Fruits in hats, oh what a scene,
Mangoes converse, 'Life's routine!'
Kiwi whispers, 'Don't be sour!'
Each enjoys the sunny hour.

Finally, they leap with glee,
Round and round, a jubilee.
Nature's laughter in the breeze,
Fruits unite with over ease!

Sunkissed Tales

Under rays where sweet dreams play,
Limes and strawberries clash in spray.
A pineapple slides on sand, oh my!
While oranges try to learn to fly.

Watermelons roll and tumble,
Finding the sun, they proudly mumble.
Cherries giggle, 'We're quite the pair!'
Hiding behind the picnic chair.

Berries dressed up in bright hues,
Tell tales of sweet, sticky snooze.
Peaches blush, 'Oh, what a find!'
As they share a love so blind.

With sugar beats, they spin around,
Each little fruit a lively sound.
In this sun, the laughter prevails,
Echoing through their sunkissed tales.

Pulp and Promise

In a blender, a wild spree,
Mango screams, 'Blend me, whee!'
Strawberries dive without a fear,
As the raspberries shout, 'Join here!'

Juicy gossip starts to swirl,
Kiwi says, 'Have you seen Pearl?'
Banana peels do laughing flips,
While oranges take tangy trips.

Pulp parties with frothy glee,
A splash of juice for you and me.
Sipping dreams from a fizzy drink,
Fruits unite, do you see the link?

Promises bubble, flavors unite,
In this blend, everything feels right.
Happiness served in a cosmic mix,
Laughter brightens the fruity fix!

The Dance of Taste

Grapefruits twirl in a sassy way,
While pears decide to join the fray.
Dancing in a juicy groove,
Every fruit has got the move.

Watermelons shake their seeds,
Bananas show off their bends and speeds.
Peaches glide with a sunset style,
Plums roll in with a cheeky smile.

Tangerines kick and jive, hooray!
As apples cheer, 'Let's seize the day!'
Nuts and berries clap along,
Join this fruity, silly song.

In the end, they find their pace,
Savoring life in every grace.
With a burst of laughter — a new taste,
A fruity dance that's never misplaced!

From Vine to Vessel

A grape was feeling quite sublime,
It dreamed of sipping aged sweet wine.
But tripping over lazy vines,
It landed flat, oh what a sign!

The farmer laughed, what a sight!
"This grape thinks it can take flight!"
With clumsy hops and silly spins,
It rolled and tumbled, lost its wins.

A bunch cheered on, they knew the score,
"Just hang in there, you'll taste much more!"
So vines entwined and then they danced,
Making juice, oh what a chance!

Then out it went, in a fancy cup,
With laughter close, they raised it up.
From vine to vessel, what a spree,
Enjoying life, so hilariously free!

The Flavorful Ascent

In an orchard high, apples plotted,
"From branch to pie, shall we be spotted?"
One said, "Let's climb, it's sure to please!"
But rolled right down, oh, what a tease!

The pears were giggling from the start,
"Just watch out for that flying cart!"
When summits passed, they faced their fate,
A fall from grace, now what's the rate?

Bananas slipped on their own peel,
In the race to meals, it was unreal!
One waved a hand, with all its might,
'We'll make it up, just hold on tight!'

Together they giggled, all in a bowl,
From orchard heights to a kitchen role.
In laughter's core, they found their flair,
With every slice, they'd rock the air!

Tales of the Tangy Path

A little lemon took a trip,
With zestful dreams and a citrus skip.
But rolling fast, it lost its way,
And wrinkled up, oh what a day!

Meanwhile, a lime just shook with glee,
Sipping on some iced tea spree.
"You'll find your path, just squeeze and roll!"
But that lemon's heart just lost control.

A berry joined in, all plump and bright,
"We'll make sweet jam, it'll be just right!"
They danced along the tangy trail,
With fruity tales that would prevail.

At last they showed, in a grand parade,
Sliced and served, oh what a trade!
With giggles sweet, they joined the fun,
Sweet stories shared, and laughter spun!

Journey of Colors and Flavors

In a garden full of bright delight,
Colors danced in morning light.
Tomatoes strutted, saying, "Look at me!"
While carrots wiggled, laughing with glee.

A pumpkin puffed, feeling quite grand,
"I'll be the star at the fall feast planned!"
But tripped on roots and rolled away,
Leaving other veggies in dismay!

Chili peppers flaunted their spicy flair,
"Join us for salsa, if you dare!"
With giggles echoed, they all set forth,
To bring their colors, to show their worth.

At last they cooked in a pot of cheer,
What a feast, they had no fear!
From garden beds to a savory glee,
They burst with laughter, deliciously free!

The Silent Symphony of Growth

In the garden, a tiny seed,
Stretched its roots in the sun's warm greed.
It danced with worms, made some friends,
Grinning wide at the twists and bends.

The rain would giggle, the soil did sigh,
Beneath a blanket of pancakes, oh my!
A sprout peeked out, a shy little guest,
Said, 'I'm here for the fun, not just to rest!'

Butterflies chuckled, birds dropped in,
'What's the joke?'—oh, where to begin?
The leaves were waving, the flowers exposed,
In nature's party, no one was dosed.

Then came the harvest, a rowdy affair,
Apples with pranks, oh, how they'd scare!
The fruit laughed aloud, 'We've grown so bold,
Join us next time, for tales yet untold!'

A Natural Tapestry

In the orchard, colors clash,
Fruits all shouted, 'Let's make a splash!'
Bananas slipped on a tangy peel,
While grapes rolled around, full of zeal.

Mangoes were chatting in juicy bliss,
While oranges played at not being missed.
The peaches giggled, plumped very proud,
Leaving lemons zinging, quite loud and wowed.

The vines were jiving, the trees went swing,
All of them waiting for the sun to bring.
Those pesky bees buzzed with cheer all day,
Just here for the nectar, in their own funny way.

At twilight's curtain, the stars turned red,
Juicy tales bumbled, stories were spread.
With winks and nods, all fruits felt bright,
'Join us next season, we'll dance through the night!'

Essence of the Orchard

In the orchard, the apples lay low,
Planning a party, with quite the show.
But pears were plotting their thoughtful pranks,
Hiding in leaves, in the flowered banks.

Cherries wore hats made of petals so rare,
Strutting their stuff without any care.
With whispers of mischief, the orchard would glow,
As fruits shared the news, 'We are ready to go!'

Plums pulled a fast one, in shades of deep blue,
Said, 'Be careful, folks, I might trust you!'
While berries debated if they were sweet,
Did they really want to be nature's treat?

The trees all chuckled, waves in the wind,
As laughter bounced, with the fun unpinned.
With blossoms all twinkling, the night dressed in flair,
They promised to meet for a fruitiest affair!

The Flow of Nature's Gifts

In gardens where giggles of veggies arise,
Tomatoes blushed, much to their surprise.
They sneaked out at night with cucumbers slim,
Planning their revels, on a fruit-filled whim.

The melons were dancing, oh, what a sight!
Swirling and twirling till dawn's early light.
Carrots brought snacks, peas made the stew,
While rhubarb recited a poem or two.

Then came the harvest, fun was afoot,
Everyone merry, no sign of a root.
They tossed in the air, laughing with glee,
Wishing to savor their jubilee spree!

Now with baskets full, onto markets they strolled,
Each winked and grinned, their stories retold.
'Join us next time; there'll be more to claim,
In the garden of laughter, it's all just a game!'

Wind's Gentle Caress

A little seed did dance and sway,
In breezy winds, it loved to play.
It twirled and spun, quite full of cheer,
Not knowing soon, the ground was near.

A gust took hold, oh what a show!
It landed hard, thought it could glow.
But dirt and worms had quite the plan,
To make a feast of this brave fan.

The sun peeked down with cheeky grins,
'Get ready, little one, for spins!'
The roots dug deep, in sneaky style,
"Can I come up?" it thought a while.

Then rain fell down, a splashy treat,
It giggled loud, life felt so sweet.
Out popped a sprout with leafy hair,
"Look at me! I'm growing, fair!"

Boughs Heavy with Promise

A branch once swayed in spring's bright light,
With tiny buds, oh what a sight!
But soon it sighed, "I've much to bear,
Just look at all this springtime flair!"

As blooms turned fruit, the weight did tease,
"Hold on tight! We're off with ease!"
They wobbled here, they wobbled there,
A merry bunch with laughter rare.

The ants marched by, a bustling crew,
"Hey, look at us! We've got a view!"
But fruits would giggle, "You are near,
We're not your snacks, we're here for cheer!"

Then came a squirrel, with eyes so wide,
"Is that a snack? I cannot hide!"
The fruit replied, with laughter bright,
"Please take a nibble, we're a delight!"

The Gift of Seasons

As summer sun began to blaze,
A tiny bud sang in a haze.
But autumn's chill made it look round,
"Oh dear, I hope I do not drown!"

The leaves turned gold, the air grew crisp,
"Hey there, fruit! Don't take a lisp!"
The whispers spread among the trees,
"Let's make a dance; it's such a tease!"

A gust swept in, like swirling glee,
"Catch me if you can, just see!"
The fruits rolled down, in merry haste,
"Who knew we could have so much taste?"

Winter brought a snowy cloak,
Where fruits told tales, and laughter broke.
"Let's hibernate till springtime sings,
And then we'll dance on blossomed wings!"

Hues of Earth and Sky

In gardens bright with colors grand,
A merry sight across the land.
The fruits all boasted, each unique,
"I'm juicy sweet! Come take a peek!"

With hues of red and shades of green,
They partied hard, a lively scene.
"Let's make a juice that glows like light,
And dance together through the night!"

As bees buzzed in to join the fun,
"Do you all mind if we get none?"
But fruits just laughed, "We've enough cheer,
Come sip and buzz, the best is near!"

So under skies of pure delight,
The fruits embraced the starry night.
In shades of joy, they'd spin and twirl,
A fruity dance, a vibrant whirl!

Ripening Under the Sun

Once a berry, tiny and round,
Hanging out where sunlight's found.
Got a tan on my skin, what a sight!
Had to dodge birds in midflight!

Laughing with lemons up in the tree,
Grapes whispering, "Come hang with me!"
Sunshine troubles? Not a care,
Just sweet times, if you dare!

Peaches giggle, their fuzz in the breeze,
Dancing with figs, oh please, oh please!
Swaying to tunes, a fruity jam,
"Who needs a coat? We're ripe, oh man!"

As the day ends with a warm embrace,
We toast the sun with a cheeky face.
Bouncing berries, here's the fun,
Ready or not, we're ripening, son!

A Journey of Flavor

A little seed starts casual and small,
Dreaming of heights, oh so tall.
With roots down deep, it grows and stirs,
While ants debate their next big spur!

Cherries chat with their husky friends,
Bouncing laughs as the fun extends.
"My skin is bright, I'm a real looker!"
"I'm tangy and fresh, I'm no mere cooker!"

Tomatoes tumble and roll in delight,
"Just wait till we're cooked, we'll ignite!"
With spices and herbs, oh what a mix,
Creating dishes with ninja tricks!

So here's the scoop from the produce aisle,
Fruits unite to make us all smile.
A riot of flavor, a funky dance,
With every crunch, let's take a chance!

Nectar in the Air

Buzzing bees with a fruity flair,
Whisking nectar, oh what a care!
Grapefruit giggles, "I'm quite a zest!"
"Join me for breakfast, I'm the best!"

Mangoes swaying, sunny and bright,
Chillin' in the orchard, what a sight!
Add in some lime, and shake it around,
With flair like a dance, we're nectar-bound!

Pineapples sport crowns, feeling so bold,
Telling tall tales of sweetness untold.
Worrying not about fruit flies near,
"Just a bit of buzz, no need to fear!"

Come join the fun, fruity parade,
Dancing and laughing, all plans well laid.
From blossoms to cocktails, we play our part,
With nectar in the air, we've got heart!

Seeds in the Wind

Winds whisper secrets to seeds at play,
"Catch a ride, don't be shy, okay?"
Off they go on a playful spree,
"To places unknown, come dance with me!"

Pumpkin seeds, round and so bright,
Floating off through the breezy night.
Squirrels scurry, their eyes so wide,
"Free gourmet meals? Oh, we'll decide!"

Apples tumble, touching the ground,
Wishing for adventure all around.
"Let's roll and shout, what a sweet thrill!
With every bounce, we'll climb that hill!"

As the sun sets, shadows grow long,
Seeds sing their funny, fruity song.
Spread the laughter, let's begin again,
For seeds in the wind, there's just no end!

From Heart to Harvest

In a garden lush and bright,
Fruits giggle in the daylight.
With dreams of pies and smoothies grand,
They plot their escape from the land.

Oranges roll, with zest and glee,
While apples chat beneath the tree.
'We're off!' they cry, so loud and clear,
To find their place in a fancy cheer.

Bananas slip with laughter bold,
Daring tales of adventures told.
'To the kitchen!' they all chant,
Imagining a fruit salad rant.

But in the bowl, a battle forms,
As fruit salad breaks all norms.
'Not too sweet!' the lemon beams,
While cherries plot in fruity dreams.

The Taste of Time

Tick-tock goes the fruit parade,
Each waiting for their sweet upgrade.
Granny Smith bides her time,
While seeing red is quite sublime.

Peaches blush, they know what's next,
In pies and tarts, they feel quite vexed.
'Is it time?', the berries plead,
'For joy or jam, we'll surely lead!'

Lemons sulk, a sour surprise,
As limes wink with playful eyes.
'Mix us up and shake it right,
We'll dance in drinks, oh what a sight!'

Oh, how they laugh in the fridge so cold,
Playing games as their tales unfold.
Time ticks on, they're ripe with glee,
Imagining their fruity jubilee!

In the Shadow of the Tree

Underneath the leafy crown,
Fruits gather round, not wearing frown.
Discussions spark, like sun rays bright,
About who'll be the first in sight.

The pear jokes, 'I'm shaped just right!'
While grapes bubble with delight.
'We'll hang out here, just wait and see,
Until it's time for our grand jubilee!'

Melons tell tales of summer fun,
Laughing about the games they've spun.
'Water fights and juicy splashes,
It's a fruit life full of fun and clashes!'

But in that shade, they all agree,
Life is good, they can be free.
With laughter rich and spirits high,
The shadowed tree, their glorious sky.

Rain's Gift to the Earth

Raindrops come with a splish and splash,
Fruits rejoice in the muddy mash.
'Here comes the party!' the cherries cheer,
As droplets dance, they gather near.

Berries bounce in puddles round,
Happily laughing without a sound.
'Let's soak it up, it's pure delight!'
While cucumbers giggle at their sight.

Rain whispered sweetly, "Grow in style!"
Fruits can't help but grin and smile.
'We're on our way, we'll soon be great,
Flaunting flavors on every plate!'

As clouds drift by and the sun peeks through,
The garden blooms in vibrant hue.
With laughter ringing in leafy lanes,
Rain's warm hugs, their joyful gains!

Drop of Nectar

From blossom bright, I take my dive,
A rain of joy, how I arrive!
I bounce and roll, oh what a ride,
Sweet sticky fun, I'm filled with pride.

I dodge a bee, it starts to buzz,
Oh no, not him! I'll start to fuzz!
With sticky fingers, I'm quite the treat,
In this world of chaos, I won't retreat.

I plop on ground, oh what a scene,
With ants in line, I'm quite the queen!
They hoot and cheer, it's quite the game,
I'll drop my seeds, they'll get the fame!

A giggle here, a squish to there,
The trees all sway, they lift my stare.
From bloom to drop, it's laughter galore,
Join me in fun, let's spread some more!

Drop of Time

Tick tock goes the clock, so divine,
A citrus splash, in a twist of lime.
With every tick, I'm full of zest,
A fruity dance, I give my best.

Day turns to night, in hues so grand,
A peach on the vine, it starts to stand.
Wobble and roll, oh what a plot,
I'm stuck in the sun, so nice and hot!

With each second, I gather some cheer,
A taste of sunshine, crystal clear.
In every moment, I feel so fine,
Ripened laughter, tucked in a line.

Through tangled vines, I roam so free,
A banana chase, come chase with me!
From blossom to wise, the clock ticks laughter,
Let's peel away, it's happily ever after!

Melodies of Maturation

Once a bud, now a cheeky sprite,
Swaying on branches, oh what a sight!
In the breeze, we laugh and sway,
A fruity tune that steals the day.

I'm ripe with jokes, and puns galore,
From nutty acorns to mangoes' roar.
As hummingbirds hum, I'll churn and dance,
Who knew growing up held such romance?

From flowers bright, to colors bold,
This fruity tale will never grow old.
Each twist and turn, a giggle in tow,
As we ripen through the fun, oh what a show!

Time slips by, oh watch me balloon,
I'll break the silence, like a fruit-filled tune.
With juicy laughter, and smiles abound,
In fruity melodies, joy is found!

Picking Moments

In a sunny field, I spot my chance,
To pluck some joy, and skip a dance.
With basket full, I chuckle loud,
For fruity treasures, I feel so proud!

I see a berry, all blue and round,
In this tasty game, I'm glory bound.
Each squishy pick, a giggle shared,
With every grab, a treasure declared.

From apples bright to grapes that twine,
I gather giggles, one at a time.
Fruits line up for their moment to shine,
Oh what a harvest, oh how divine!

With every lift and every stash,
I bubble with joy, oh the sweet sweet cache!
As laughter echoes, I take a bow,
In this patch of fun, let's pick it now!

Ferns and Fruition

Among the ferns, a secret lies,
A fruity dream beneath the skies.
With roots so deep, and hearts so light,
In nature's hands, we take our flight.

A merry dance in the forest green,
With every twist, a forest scene.
The fruits are laughing, their giggles bright,
In ferns we find our pure delight!

From stubborn seeds to leaps of joy,
Fruition and fun, we dare deploy.
A mischievous breeze, it tickles my leaves,
In shades of green, it all believes.

So let's sway along, in this lilting song,
In nature's tune, where we belong.
With every sprout and every cheer,
In ferns and fruits, the joy is near!

The Art of Becoming

In a garden where sweetness awaits,
A berry once dreamed of grand dinner plates.
It hoped for adventures, fun just the same,
Dressed up in sunshine and playing the game.

A banana once slipped on its own peel,
Cried out, "Hey folks, this is part of the deal!"
Told all the citrus, "You should join in!"
With a zesty parade, let the laughter begin!

An apple, quite round, with a glossy face,
Said to a grape, "I could win a race!"
With pit stops for juice and a laugh on the way,
They rolled towards the market, brightening the day!

From blossom to banquet, they giggled in glee,
With each little pitfall that set them all free.
"We're fruit of the fun, with stories to share,
Join in our harvest, there's joy everywhere!"

Sojourn of the Seeds

Tiny seeds start their wild little quest,
Dreams planted deep, they long for a jest.
They wriggled and giggled, each sprout of green,
"Where will we end up? What will we glean?"

A watermelon whispered, "I want to be king!
In summer cool shade, I'll throw the best fling!"
The cucumbers chuckled, "We shall be quite cool,
Dressed in our stripes like we're heading to school!"

As sprouts they would dance in the warm sunny light,
Each leaf made them laugh, what a wonderful sight!
They did little spins, spinning round and round,
With giggles that echoed throughout the ground.

When harvest finally called, they were quite the show,
From patch to the table, in a colorful flow.
"From seed to delight, what a raucous ride!
Join the party, friends, let's give it some pride!"

A Symphony of Succulence

Fruits gathered round for a vibrant soirée,
A peach took the lead, "Let's dance and not sway!"
With rhythms of juice and a beat made of zest,
They jived 'til the stars made the night feel impressed.

"Play the flute, Mr. Fig," called a sweet tangerine,
"Let's samba with gusto, it'll be quite the scene!"
Cherries were twirling and lemons flipped high,
While apples and berries joined in, oh my!

A pineapple burst in, "I've got disco moves!"
As papayas clapped hands, and each fruit disapproves,
Of dullness and drab, they raise the fruit scale,
Taking their talents to berry-tastic trails!

As morning approached, kids feasted with cheer,
On fruity confetti that brightened the sphere.
Together they sang of their fun-filled night,
With laughter and sweetness, oh what a sight!

The Colors of Ripeness

A lemon felt ripe as it donned a bright hue,
Challenged a lime, "Can you top this debut?"
The orange chimed in with its vibrant flair,
"Let's zest up this party; we'll taste, if we dare!"

A mango exclaimed, "I'm the sweetest delight,
Careful, my friends, to not take a bite!"
The berries then giggled, "We're small but we pack,
A punch of fun flavor; there's never a lack!"

As colors collided, a canvas was made,
Of smoothies and salads in bright masquerade.
With laughter around and a splash of confetti,
Fruit art in the bowl? Oh, it's looking so petty!

At the end of the day, they all took a bow,
With flavors so lively, they'd steal your heart now.
In this feast of colors, so juicy and bright,
The fruits shared their joy, shining day and night!

From Blossom to Bounty

Oh, little bud, so fresh and bright,
You giggle as you soak in light.
With petals wide, you start the dance,
While bees all buzz, and bugs take a chance.

Growing round, you start to swell,
A jolly round ball, you know it well.
Sunshine drips from every hue,
You're a snack that's waiting for the chew!

Oh, the day you drop with flair,
A plop on grass, with not a care!
The world erupts in laughs and cheers,
As munchies gather through the years!

In pie or jam, you find your fame,
With every bite, you win the game!
A journey full of tasty glee,
Who knew the fruit could be so free?

In the Orchard's Embrace

In the orchard's shade, ripe tales unfold,
Where apples chuckle, and pears are bold.
They tell jokes of worms and bees,
While hanging out among the leaves.

Peaches wear blushing gowns of fluff,
They ponder life and all that stuff.
"Why are we so sweet?" one asks with pride,
"Because the sun is our silky guide!"

Beneath the boughs, the laughter hums,
As fruit gets silly, and nobody shuns.
"Let's roll down the hill!" a grape would shout,
And off they go, a jellybean rout!

In the basket, their giggles remain,
Sharing stories, teasing rain.
Together they bask in nature's art,
In the orchard's laugh, they'll never part!

Whispers of Ripeness

Among the leaves, secrets are stirred,
A raspberry speaks, but only to birds.
"Can you believe, I'm almost ripe?"
The strawberries giggle, "You'll soon be hype!"

Bananas joke, "We're tired of green,
We want to wear yellow, like the sunbeam!"
The oranges chime in, "We're juicy and bright,
Our zest brings all the bees to the light!"

So they plot all day in fruity delight,
To catch a breeze and take to flight.
With every whisper, a plan takes shape,
As each awaits their perfect escape!

Just one more day in the sun's embrace,
They'll laugh and roll at a speedy pace.
From tree to table, what a parade,
The whispers of ripeness, a bold charade!

Through Thorn and Bramble

A berry bold, a raspberry brave,
Dared to wander where the thorns wave.
"I'm fine!" it cried, with a wink and a giggle,
But thorns had plans, to shake and to wiggle!

"I'll make it through, I'm tough as nails!"
Yet every twist, it tells tall tales.
With branches scratching, a fruit's ballet,
The dance of wits on a wild ballet!

Through bramble and bush, oh what a sight,
A two-step stumble, a tumble, a fright!
But laughter rings, as it lands with a thud,
With nature's embrace, it's covered in mud!

At last on the path, it finds a way,
To bask in the sun, for a fun-filled day.
With juicy laughter that breaks past the wall,
A berry's adventure—the funniest of all!

Cider Wind and Orchard Tales

In an orchard so sweet, apples decide,
To ride on the breeze, with nothing to hide.
They giggle and bounce on the branches so high,
Cider dreams swirling, they burst with a sigh.

The pears join the fun, with a swing and a sway,
They slip and they slide, in the sunlight's play.
"Watch us now!" they shout, as they tumble on down,
With laughter and juice, they're the talk of the town.

The apricots dance with a twist and a twirl,
While peaches make faces, their fuzz in a whirl.
Together they frolic, in playful debate,
"Who's juicier?" they yell, as they all celebrate!

When the day finally ends, with a sunset so bright,
They roll to the basket, their dreams taking flight.
With smiles in their cores, they embrace the delight,
For tomorrow awaits, with more fun in sight.

The Quest for Sunlit Splendor

Under the sun, berries all seek,
Their journey begins, with a giggle and squeak.
They scamper and scatter, each one in a race,
To find the best spot, in this bright, happy place.

The grapes make a pact, in a cluster so tight,
"We're off to the vineyard, it'll be quite a sight!"
They bounce on the leaves, in the warm, golden ray,
Sharing silly tales of a fruit salad play.

The cherries, they chatter, while dangling in glee,
"Look at us shining, like gems on a tree!"
With a flip and a flop, they reach for the sun,
Declaring together, "This ripening's fun!"

As the sun starts to set, they gather around,
With fruit punch like laughter, and joy that's profound.
They toast to their travels, with smiles all aglow,
What a quest it has been, oh what a show!

Roots and Roads Unraveled

Little carrots peek out, from their cozy deep beds,
"We're looking for sunshine, and maybe some threads!"
With roots full of humor, they wiggle and play,
Lively little veggies, who brighten the day.

Onions join in, with a tearful delight,
"We'll follow the path, till we reach the high light!"
With layers of laughter, they're ready to roll,
Each twist and each turn brings out their good soul.

Potatoes all chuckle, as they loosen their skins,
"In this muddy adventure, we're destined for wins!"
They trip on their tops, in a dance like no other,
Together they giggle, like sister and brother.

As they finally sprout, in the sun's warm embrace,
They relish the journey, their newfound grace.
With roots all entwined, they claim victory mere,
For growing together is the joy they hold dear.

From Seedling to Feast

Oh the little seedlings, how they dream big,
Wishing to grow up, and dance like a jig.
They poke through the soil, with hopes that are bright,
Imagining feasts in the warm, sunny light.

As sunshine arrives, they stretch and they spin,
"Just wait till we're veggies, let the feast begin!"
Each leaf joins in chorus, with rustles and cheer,
Creating a salad that all can hold dear.

Radishes chuckle, "We're spicy and bold,
We'll add to the mix, turning young green to gold!"
Then tomatoes chip in, with their juicy delight,
"We'll splash in some color, make everything right!"

At last comes the day, when they all gather 'round,
In bowls full of laughter, with scents that astound.
From seedlings to feast, with a fun-loving crew,
What a funny journey, they all made it through!

www.ingramcontent.com/pod-product-compliance
Lightning Source LLC
Chambersburg PA
CBHW070304120526
44590CB00017B/2562